Building Sentences

MADE FUN

Growing Minds

PRESS

Visit Us Online

Download Free Printables

growingmindspress.wixsite.com/home

Follow us on social media:

Benefits of This Book

✓ Provides practice with the important Kindergarten skill of building sentences for a solid writing foundation

✓ Provides sentence scramble practice using sight words to build grade level appropriate sentences

✓ Movable pieces help children unscramble sentences

✓ Self-check sentence reminders reinforce proper sentence formation

✓ Builds on sentence practice by adding details to improve the sentence and make it longer

✓ Question prompts help learners develop ideas for building longer sentences

✓ Optional prompts assist with sentence formation when necessary

✓ Starting dots on each letter help reinforce correct letter formation

✓ Starting dot on handwriting lines help reinforce starting on the far left when writing

Sentence Scrambles Instructions

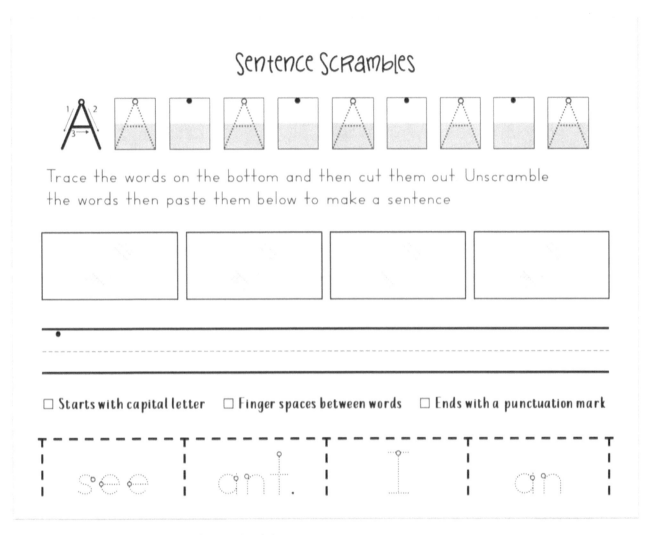

1. Trace and copy the letter.
2. Trace the words on the bottom strip.
3. Cut out the long part of the strip.
4. Snip the short parts of the strip.
5. Rearrange the words to make a sentence.
   1. Tip: Sentences start with a capital letter, so put the word that starts with a capital letter first.
   2. Tip: Sentences end with punctuation marks, so put the word that ends with a punctuation mark last.
6. Glue the words to the boxes.
7. Copy the sentence using the dot as a guide for where to start writing.
8. Check the self-check items and mark the boxes.

Sentence Stretching Instructions

SENTENCE STRETCHING

Stretch the sentence from the previous page.

I see an ant and a

What else do you see? Copy the phrase and add another detail to make your sentence.

☐ Starts with capital letter   ☐ Finger spaces between words   ☐ Ends with a punctuation mark

Optional Prompts:

worm   ladybug   snail

1. Trace and copy the phrase.
2. Read the question to help think of how to add more detail to make a longer sentence.
   1. Tip: Optional prompts are located towards the bottom of the page. Some learners may come up with ideas without using the prompts, whereas other children will find the prompts helpful. Follow your child's lead, and provide them with the prompts if they need them so they don't become frustrated or discouraged.
3. Copy the phrase and include the added word(s) to make your sentence longer.
4. Check the self-check items and mark the boxes.

Sentence Scrambles

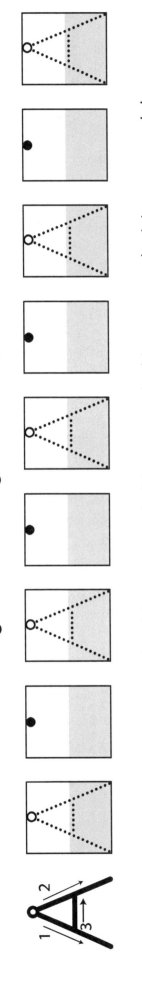

Trace the words on the bottom and then cut them out. Unscramble the words then paste them below to make a sentence.

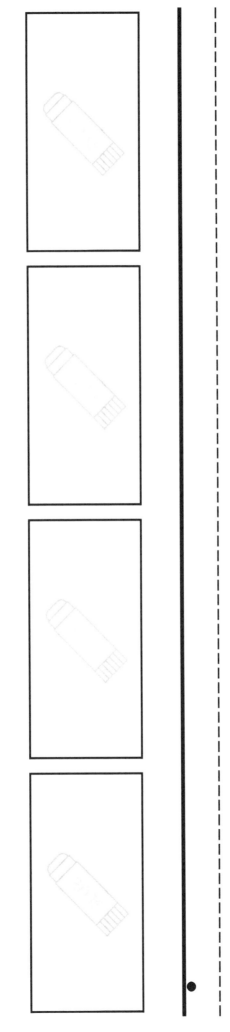

☐ Starts with capital letter   ☐ Finger spaces between words   ☐ Ends with a punctuation mark

FIRST TRACE BELOW THEN CUT HERE

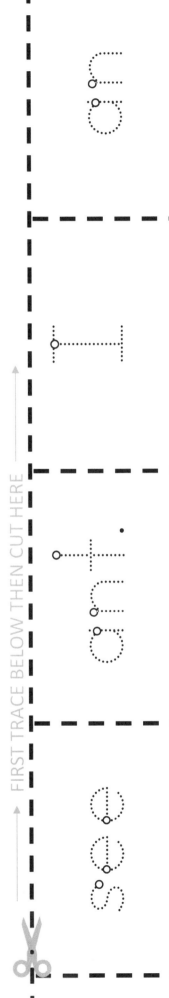

SENTENCE STRETCHING

Stretch the sentence from the previous page.

I see an ant and a

What else do you see? Copy the phrase and add another detail to make your sentence.

•

_____

_____

☐ Starts with capital letter   ☐ Finger spaces between words

☐ Ends with a punctuation mark

Optional Prompts:

worm.   ladybug.   snail.

Sentence Scrambles

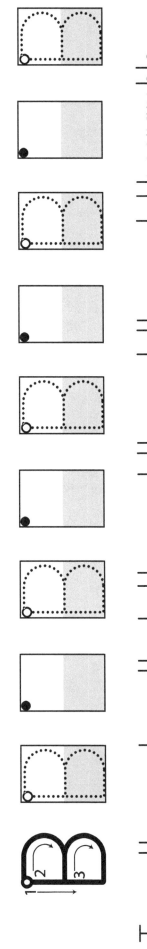

Trace the words on the bottom and then cut them out. Unscramble the words then paste them below to make a sentence.

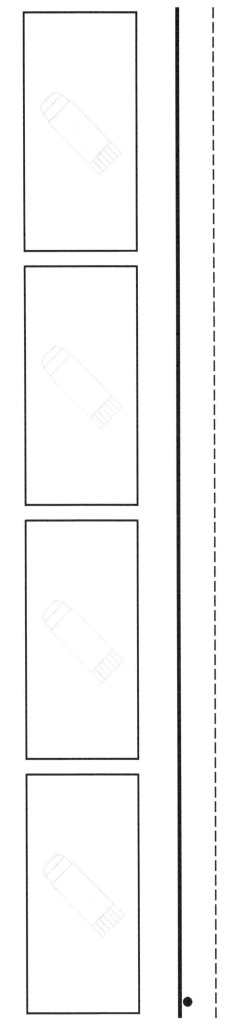

☐ Starts with capital letter ☐ Finger spaces between words ☐ Ends with a punctuation mark

FIRST TRACE BELOW THEN CUT HERE

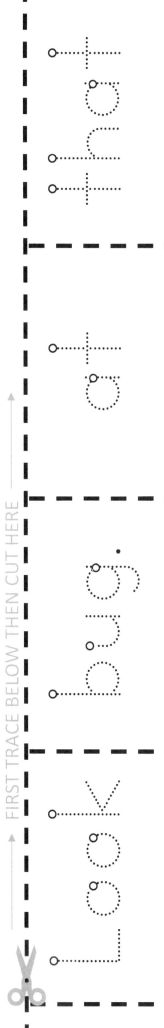

Look bug. at that

SENTENCE STRETCHING

Stretch the sentence from the previous page.

Look at that bug on the

Where is the bug? Copy the phrase and add another detail to make your sentence.

● _ _ _ _ _ _ _ _ _ _ _

━━━━━━━━━━━━━━

━━━━━━━━━━━━━━

━━━━━━━━━━━━━━

☐ Starts with capital letter   ☐ Finger spaces between words

☐ Ends with a punctuation mark

Optional Prompts:
window.   leaf.   car.

Sentence Scrambles

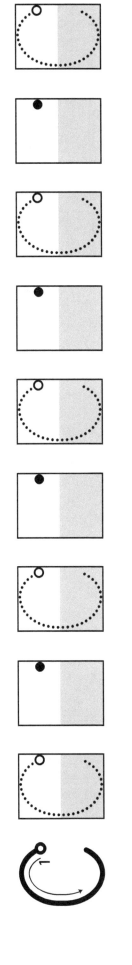

Trace the words on the bottom and then cut them out. Unscramble the words then paste them below to make a sentence.

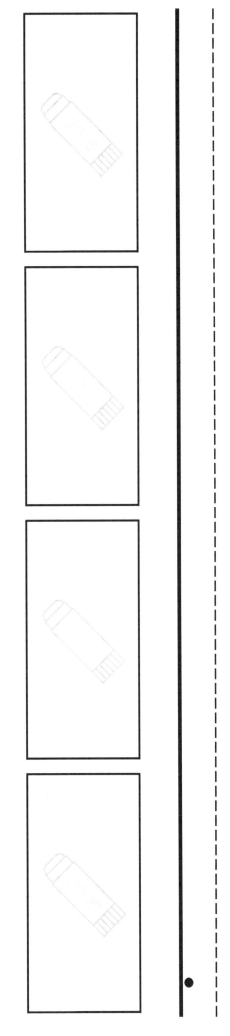

☐ Starts with capital letter   ☐ Finger spaces between words   ☐ Ends with a punctuation mark

✂ FIRST TRACE BELOW THEN CUT HERE

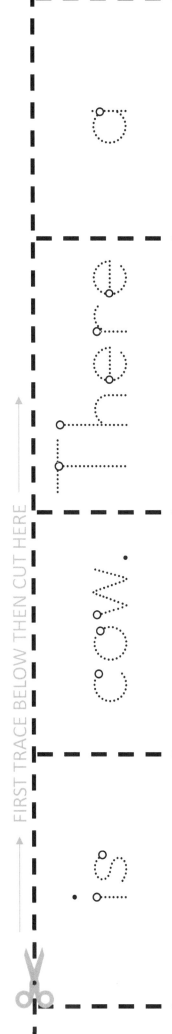

SENTENCE STRETCHING

Stretch the sentence from the previous page.

There is a cow.

What is the cow doing? Copy the phrase and add another detail to make your sentence.

•

_____

- - - - - - - - - - - - - - - -

_____

_____

☐ **Starts with capital letter**   ☐ **Finger spaces between words**

☐ **Ends with a punctuation mark**

Optional Prompts:
eating grass.   sleeping.   mooing.

Sentence Scrambles

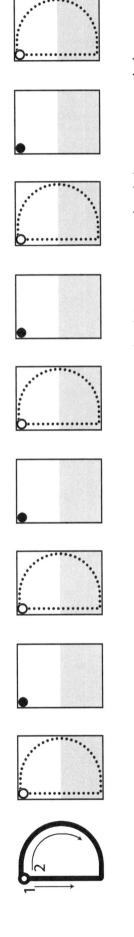

Trace the words on the bottom and then cut them out. Unscramble the words then paste them below to make a sentence.

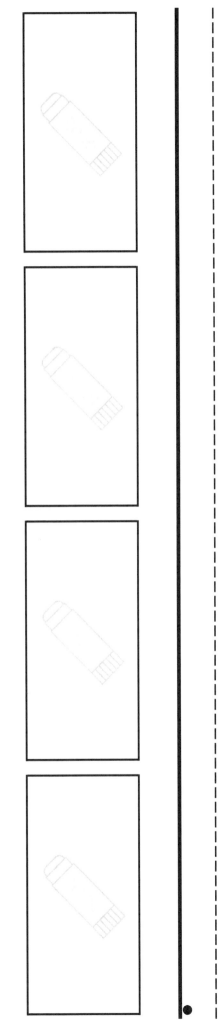

□ Starts with capital letter   □ Finger spaces between words   □ Ends with a punctuation mark

FIRST TRACE BELOW THEN CUT HERE

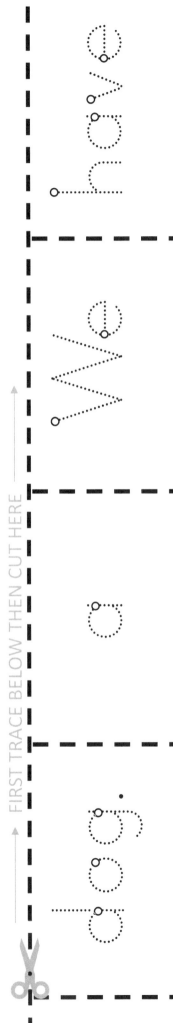

SENTENCE STRETCHING

Stretch the sentence from the previous page.

We have a dog.

What kind of dog is it? Copy the phrase and add another detail to make your sentence.

•

- - - - - - - -

☐ Starts with capital letter   ☐ Finger spaces between words   ☐ Ends with a punctuation mark

Optional Prompts:
little   big   white

Sentence Scrambles

Trace the words on the bottom and then cut them out. Unscramble the words then paste them below to make a sentence.

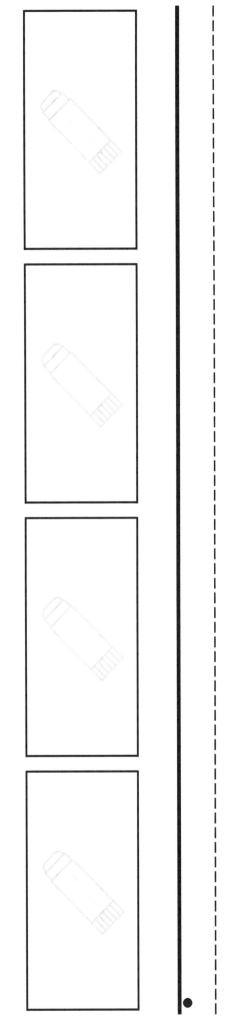

☐ Starts with capital letter ☐ Finger spaces between words ☐ Ends with a punctuation mark

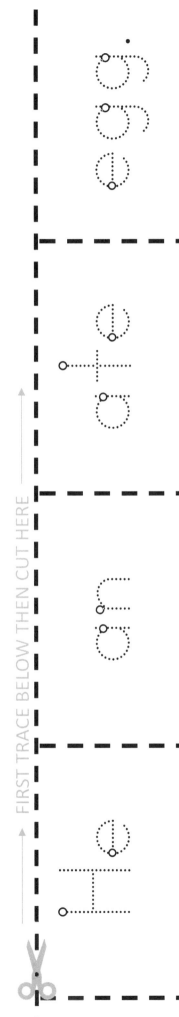

Stretch the sentence from the previous page.

He ate an egg and

What else did he eat? Copy the phrase and add another detail to make your sentence.

☐ Starts with capital letter   ☐ Finger spaces between words   ☐ Ends with a punctuation mark

Optional Prompts:

toast.   bacon.   sausage.

Sentence Scrambles

Trace the words on the bottom and then cut them out. Unscramble the words then paste them below to make a sentence.

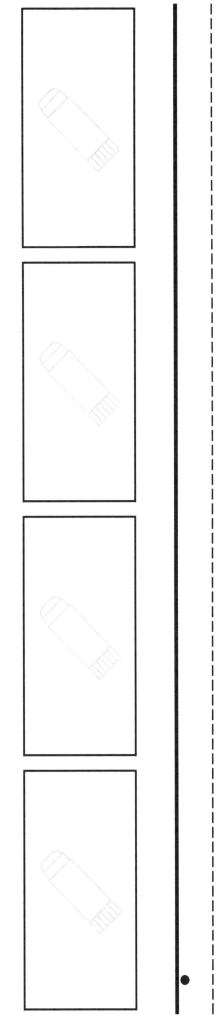

☐ Starts with capital letter   ☐ Finger spaces between words   ☐ Ends with a punctuation mark

FIRST TRACE BELOW THEN CUT HERE

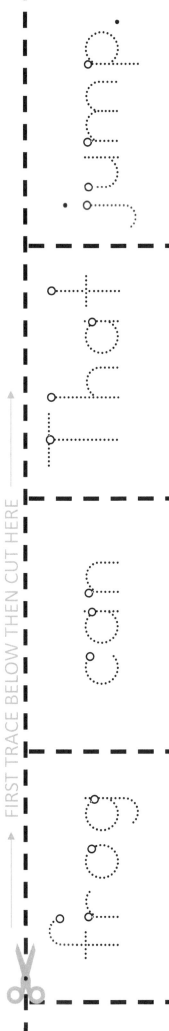

SENTENCE STRETCHING

Stretch the sentence from the previous page.

That frog can jump .

Where did the frog jump? Copy the phrase and add another detail to make your sentence.

-

- - - - - - -

☐ **Starts with capital letter**   ☐ **Finger spaces between words**   ☐ **Ends with a punctuation mark**

Optional Prompts:
in the water.   over the log.   in the grass.
in the water.   in the grass.

Sentence Scrambles

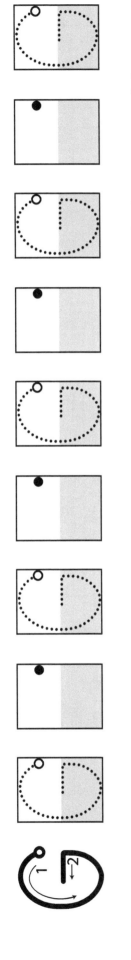

Trace the words on the bottom and then cut them out. Unscramble the words then paste them below to make a sentence.

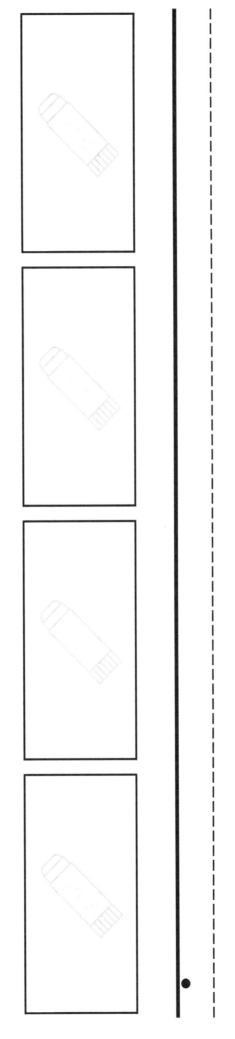

☐ Starts with capital letter ☐ Finger spaces between words ☐ Ends with a punctuation mark

FIRST TRACE BELOW THEN CUT HERE

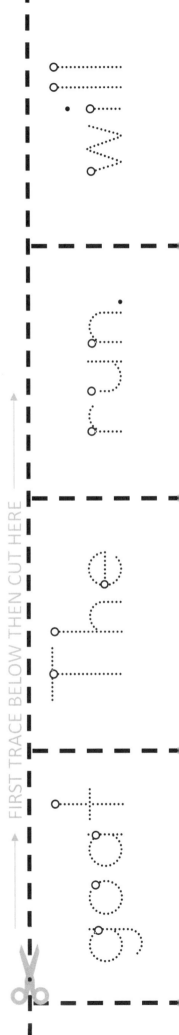

Stretch the sentence from the previous page.

The

What kind of goat is it? Copy the phrase and add another detail to make your sentence.

goat will run.

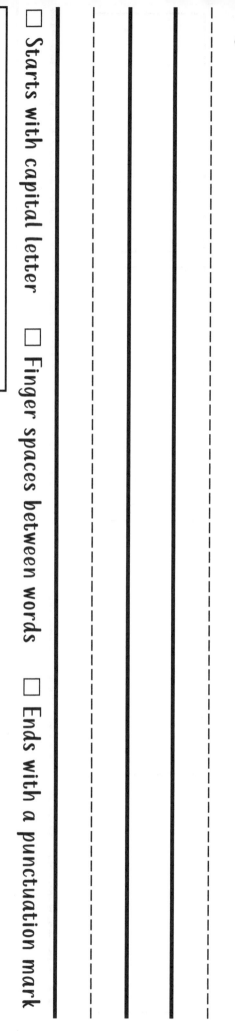

☐ Starts with capital letter   ☐ Finger spaces between words   ☐ Ends with a punctuation mark

Optional Prompts:

brown   little   baby

Sentence Scrambles

Trace the words on the bottom and then cut them out. Unscramble the words then paste them below to make a sentence.

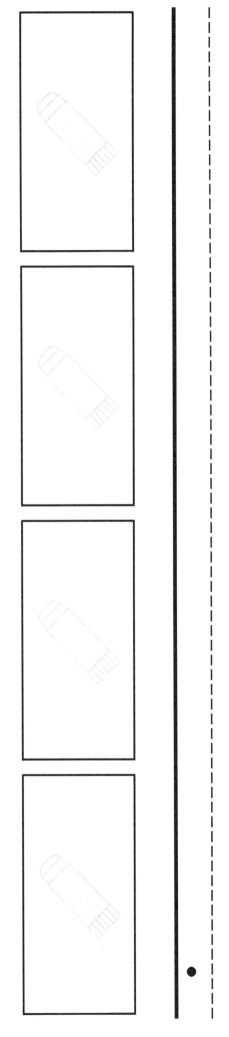

FIRST TRACE BELOW THEN CUT HERE

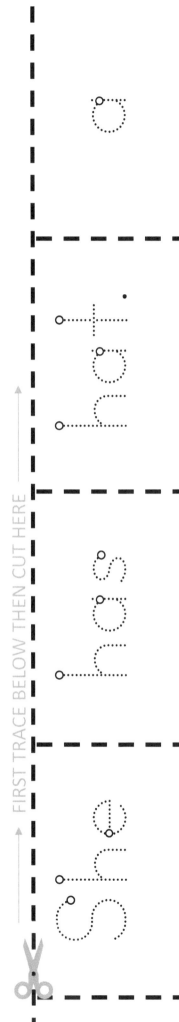

She   has   hat.   a

Stretch the sentence from the previous page.

She has a 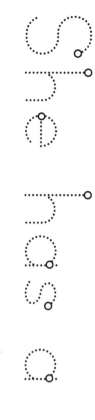 hat.

What word describes the hat? Copy the phrase and add another detail to make your sentence.

• _____

☐ Starts with capital letter   ☐ Finger spaces between words   ☐ Ends with a punctuation mark

Optional Prompts:

blue   pretty   winter

Sentence Scrambles

Trace the words on the bottom and then cut them out. Unscramble the words then paste them below to make a sentence.

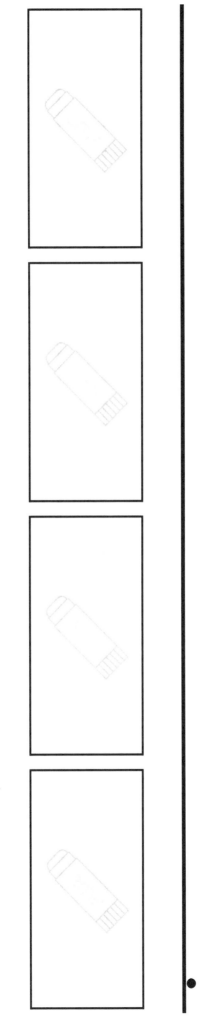

FIRST TRACE BELOW THEN CUT HERE

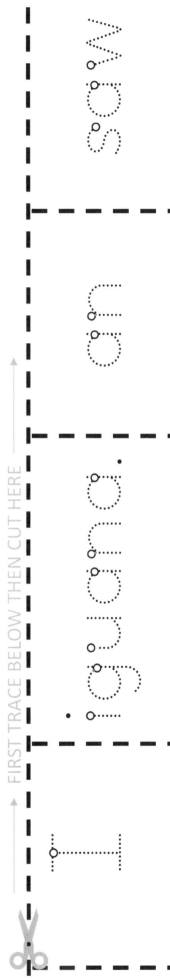

saw

an

iguana.

I

SENTENCE STRETCHING

Stretch the sentence from the previous page.

I saw an iguana.

Where was the iguana? Copy the phrase and add another detail to make your sentence.

●_____

_ _ _ _ _ _ _ _ _ _ _ _ _ _ _ _ _ _ _

_____

_____

_ _ _ _ _ _ _ _ _ _ _ _ _ _ _ _ _ _ _

☐ Starts with capital letter   ☐ Finger spaces between words   ☐ Ends with a punctuation mark

Optional Prompts:
outside.   at the zoo.   in the sand.

Sentence Scrambles

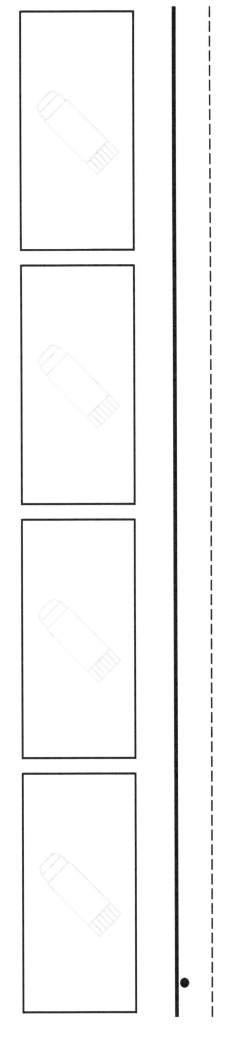

Trace the words on the bottom and then cut them out. Unscramble the words then paste them below to make a sentence.

☐ Starts with capital letter ☐ Finger spaces between words ☐ Ends with a punctuation mark

FIRST TRACE BELOW THEN CUT HERE

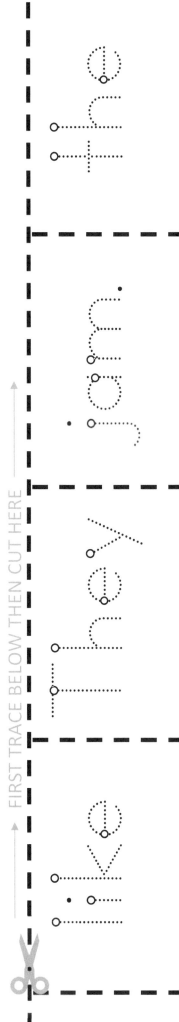

the

jam.

They

like

SENTENCE STRETCHING

Stretch the sentence from the previous page.

They like the 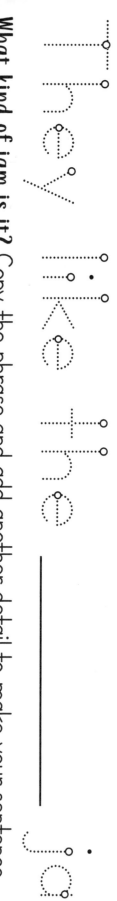 jam.

What kind of jam is it? Copy the phrase and add another detail to make your sentence.

_____

_____

_____

☐ Starts with capital letter   ☐ Finger spaces between words   ☐ Ends with a punctuation mark

Optional Prompts:
strawberry   tasty   sweet

Sentence Scrambles

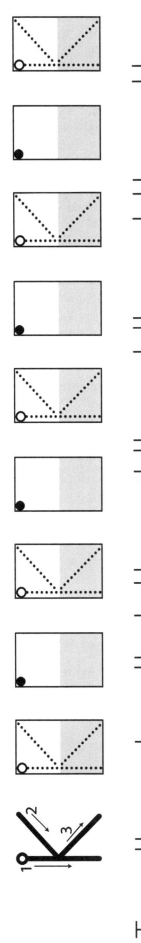

Trace the words on the bottom and then cut them out. Unscramble the words then paste them below to make a sentence.

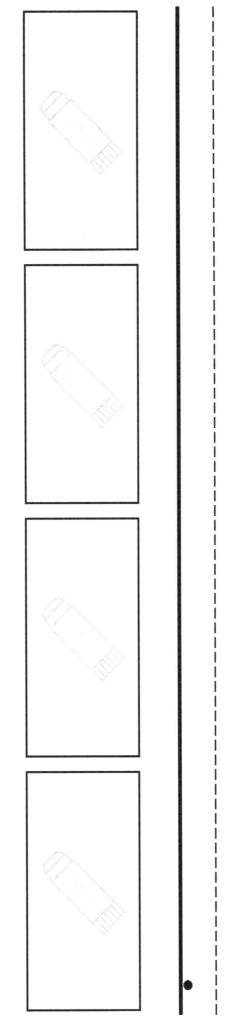

☐ Starts with capital letter ☐ Finger spaces between words ☐ Ends with a punctuation mark

FIRST TRACE BELOW THEN CUT HERE

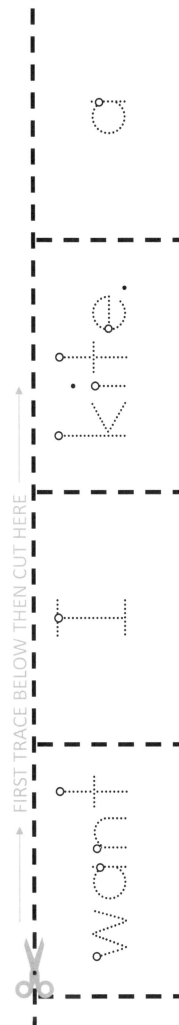

Stretch the sentence from the previous page.

I want to a kite.

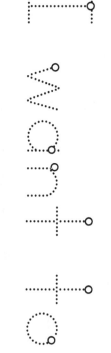

What do you want to do with the kite? Copy the phrase and add another detail to make your sentence.

☐ Starts with capital letter   ☐ Finger spaces between words   ☐ Ends with a punctuation mark

Optional Prompts:

fly   build   run with

Sentence Scrambles

Trace the words on the bottom and then cut them out. Unscramble the words then paste them below to make a sentence.

□ Starts with capital letter   □ Finger spaces between words   □ Ends with a punctuation mark

FIRST TRACE BELOW THEN CUT HERE

That   is   big   lion

SENTENCE STRETCHING

Stretch the sentence from the previous page.

That lion is big and

• _____

What else describes the lion? Copy the phrase and add another detail to make your sentence.

☐ Starts with capital letter   ☐ Finger spaces between words   ☐ Ends with a punctuation mark

Optional Prompts:
fierce.   strong.   fast.

Sentence Scrambles

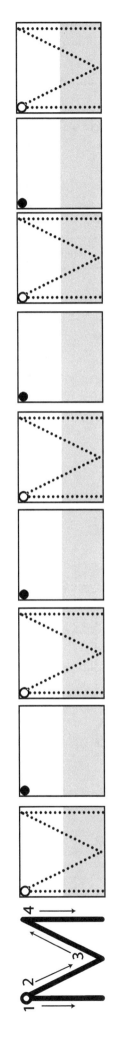

Trace the words on the bottom and then cut them out. Unscramble the words then paste them below to make a sentence.

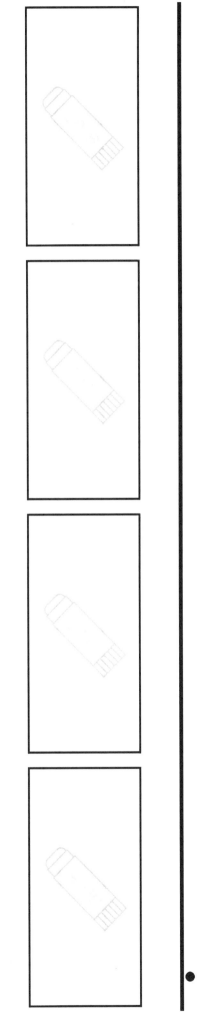

☐ Starts with capital letter ☐ Finger spaces between words ☐ Ends with a punctuation mark

← FIRST TRACE BELOW THEN CUT HERE

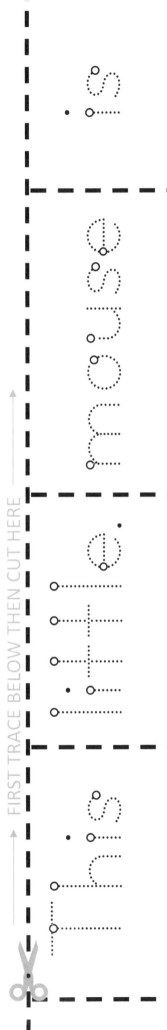

SENTENCE STRETCHING

Stretch the sentence from the previous page.

This mouse is little and

• _____

_____

_____

_____

What else describes the mouse? Copy the phrase and add another detail to make your sentence.

☐ Starts with capital letter   ☐ Finger spaces between words

☐ Ends with a punctuation mark

Optional Prompts:
quiet.   brown.   fast.

Sentence Scrambles

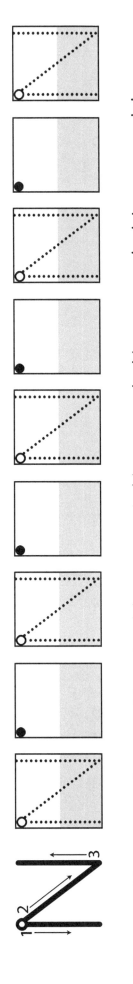

Trace the words on the bottom and then cut them out. Unscramble the words then paste them below to make a sentence.

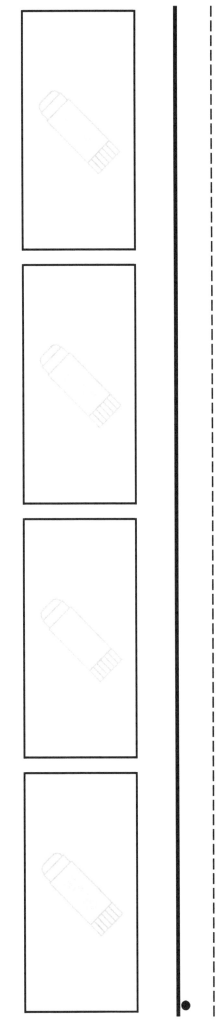

☐ Starts with capital letter ☐ Finger spaces between words ☐ Ends with a punctuation mark

FIRST TRACE BELOW THEN CUT HERE

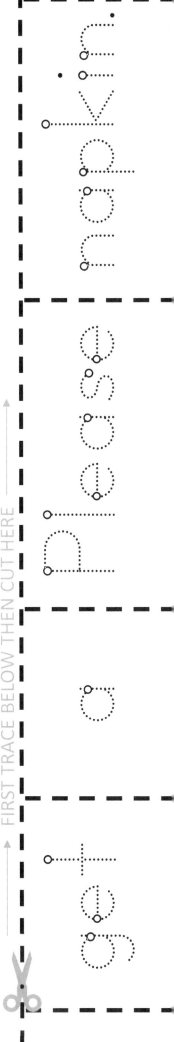

napkin

Please

a

Get

SENTENCE STRETCHING

Stretch the sentence from the previous page.

Please get a napkin to

What will you do with the napkin? Copy the phrase and add another detail to make your sentence.

- ☐ Starts with capital letter   ☐ Finger spaces between words   ☐ Ends with a punctuation mark

Optional Prompts:

wipe your hands.   wipe your face.   clean the spill.

Sentence Scrambles

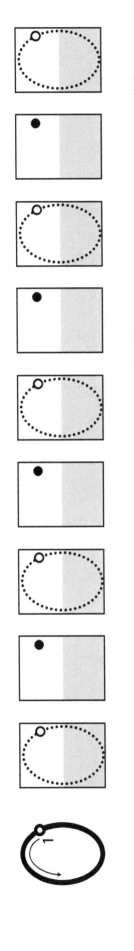

Trace the words on the bottom and then cut them out. Unscramble the words then paste them below to make a sentence.

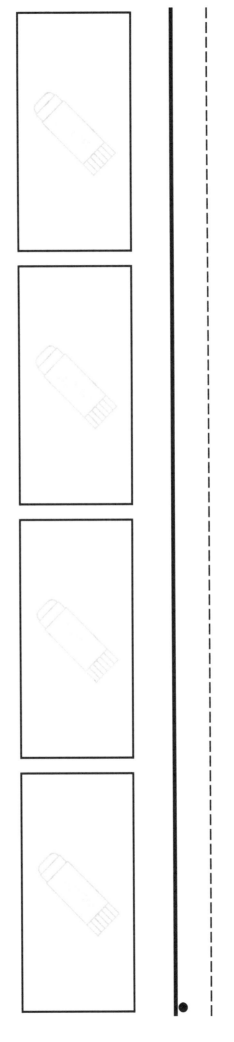

☐ Starts with capital letter ☐ Finger spaces between words ☐ Ends with a punctuation mark

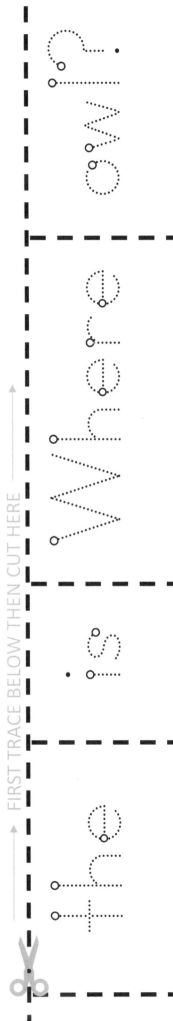

FIRST TRACE BELOW THEN CUT HERE

The   is   Where   owl?

SENTENCE STRETCHING

Stretch the sentence from the previous page.

Where is the owl?

What kind of owl is it? Copy the phrase and add another detail to make your sentence.

☐ Starts with capital letter　☐ Finger spaces between words　☐ Ends with a punctuation mark

Optional Prompts:

baby　　wise　　brown

Sentence Scrambles

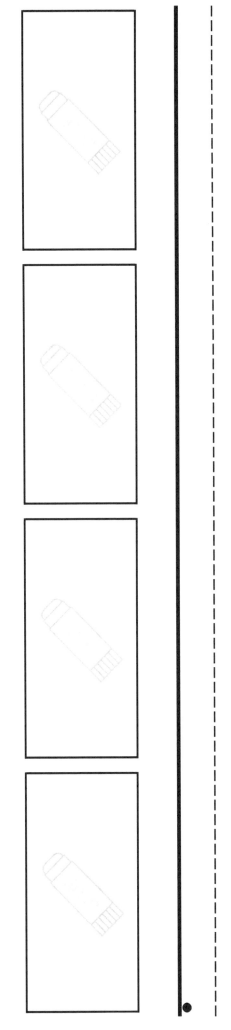

Trace the words on the bottom and then cut them out. Unscramble the words then paste them below to make a sentence.

☐ Starts with capital letter   ☐ Finger spaces between words   ☐ Ends with a punctuation mark

FIRST TRACE BELOW THEN CUT HERE

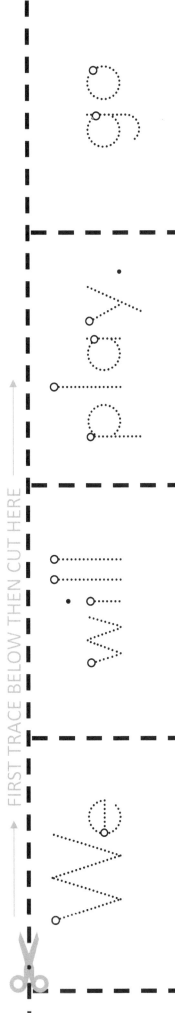

Stretch the sentence from the previous page.

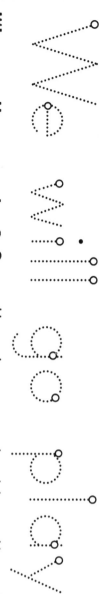

Where will we go play? Copy the phrase and add another detail to make your sentence.

☐ Starts with capital letter   ☐ Finger spaces between words   ☐ Ends with a punctuation mark

Optional Prompts:
outside.   in the yard.   at the park.

Sentence Scrambles

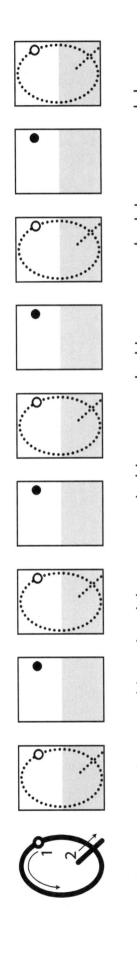

Trace the words on the bottom and then cut them out. Unscramble the words then paste them below to make a sentence.

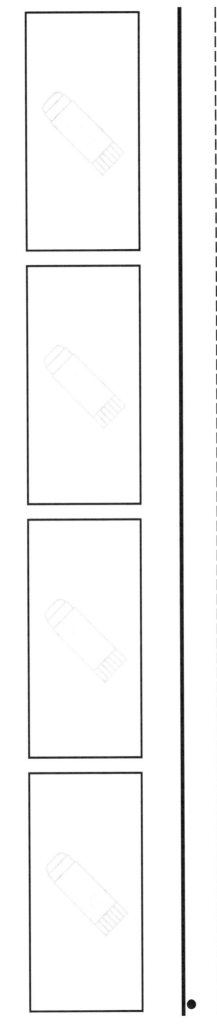

FIRST TRACE BELOW THEN CUT HERE

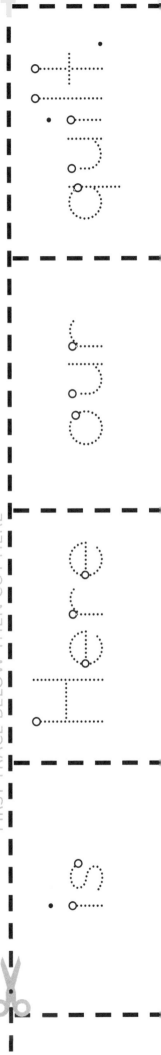

quit

out

Here

is

SENTENCE STRETCHING

Stretch the sentence from the previous page.

Here is our quilt.

What kind of quilt is it? Copy the phrase and add another detail to make your sentence.

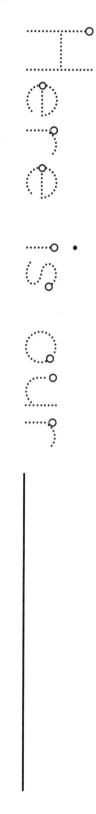

☐ Starts with capital letter   ☐ Finger spaces between words   ☐ Ends with a punctuation mark

Optional Prompts:

warm   colorful   new

Sentence Scrambles

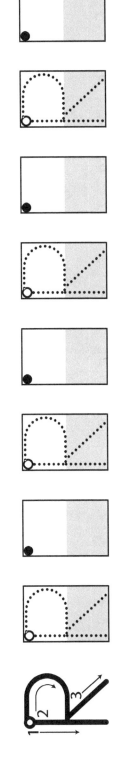

Trace the words on the bottom and then cut them out. Unscramble the words then paste them below to make a sentence.

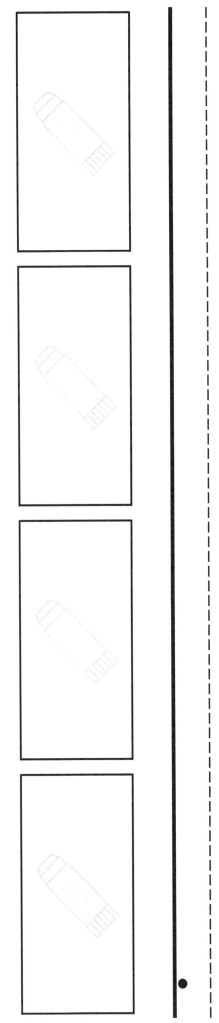

☐ Starts with capital letter   ☐ Finger spaces between words   ☐ Ends with a punctuation mark

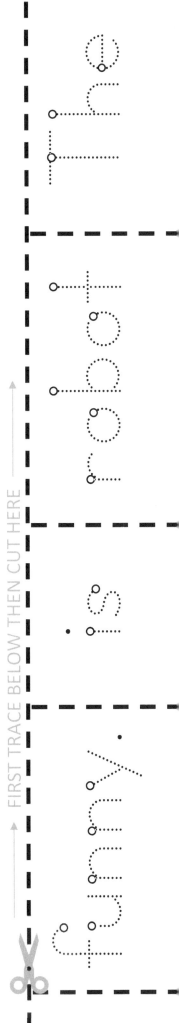

Stretch the sentence from the previous page.

The robot is funny and

What else describes the robot? Copy the phrase and add another detail to make your sentence.

•

☐ Starts with capital letter   ☐ Finger spaces between words   ☐ Ends with a punctuation mark

Optional Prompts:

smart.   nice.   quick.

Sentence Scrambles

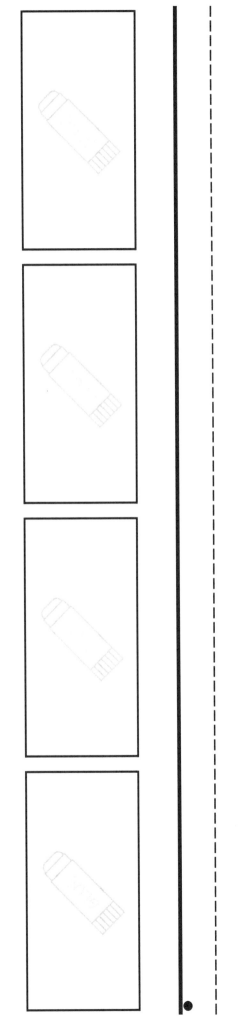

Trace the words on the bottom and then cut them out. Unscramble the words then paste them below to make a sentence.

☐ Starts with capital letter   ☐ Finger spaces between words   ☐ Ends with a punctuation mark

→ FIRST TRACE BELOW THEN CUT HERE ←

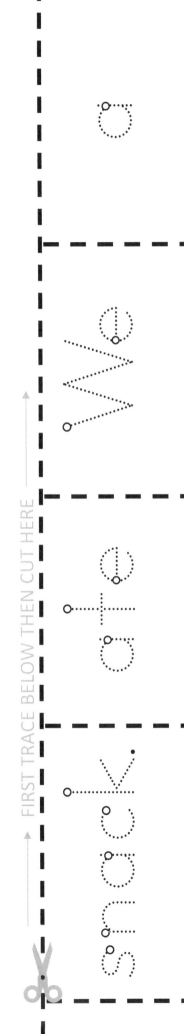

a

We

ate

snack

Stretch the sentence from the previous page.

We ate a snack after

When did you eat a snack? Copy the phrase and add another detail to make your sentence.

☐ Starts with capital letter   ☐ Finger spaces between words   ☐ Ends with a punctuation mark

Optional Prompts:
lunch.   school.   the movie.

Sentence Scrambles

Trace the words on the bottom and then cut them out. Unscramble the words then paste them below to make a sentence.

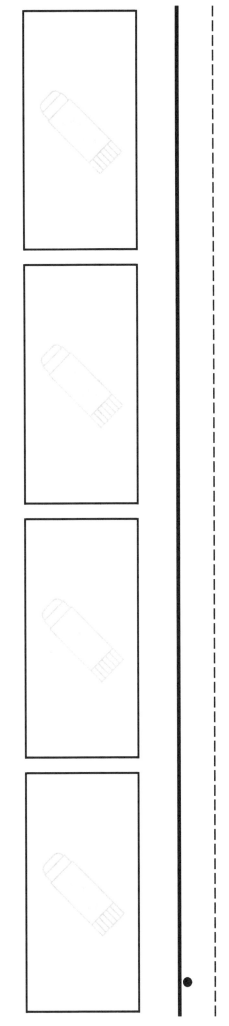

☐ Starts with capital letter   ☐ Finger spaces between words   ☐ Ends with a punctuation mark

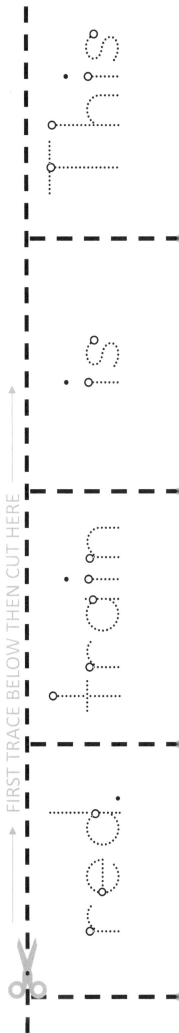

SENTENCE STRETCHING

Stretch the sentence from the previous page.

This _____ train is red.

What other word describes the train? Copy the phrase and add another detail to make your sentence.

• _____

_____

_____

☐ Starts with capital letter   ☐ Finger spaces between words

☐ Ends with a punctuation mark

Optional Prompts:
fast   big   fun

Sentence Scrambles

Trace the words on the bottom and then cut them out. Unscramble the words then paste them below to make a sentence.

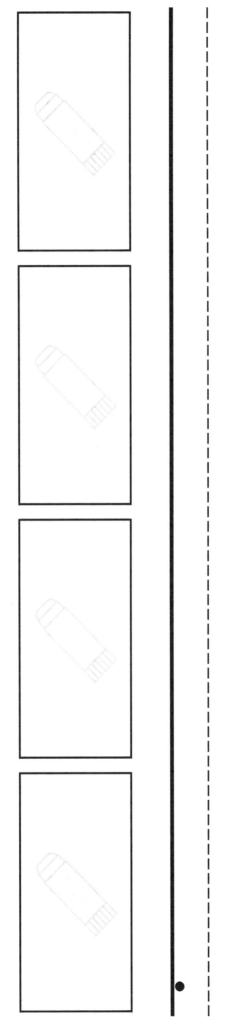

☐ Starts with capital letter ☐ Finger spaces between words ☐ Ends with a punctuation mark

FIRST TRACE BELOW THEN CUT HERE

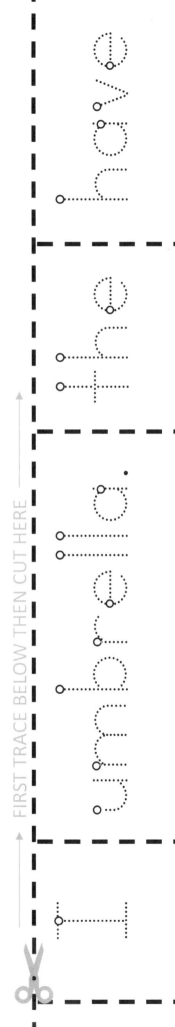

I umbrella. the have

SENTENCE STRETCHING

Stretch the sentence from the previous page.

I have the

What color is the umbrella? Copy the phrase and add another detail to make your sentence.

umbrella.

_____

_____

_____

☐ Starts with capital letter   ☐ Finger spaces between words   ☐ Ends with a punctuation mark

Optional Prompts:

blue   yellow   purple

Sentence Scrambles

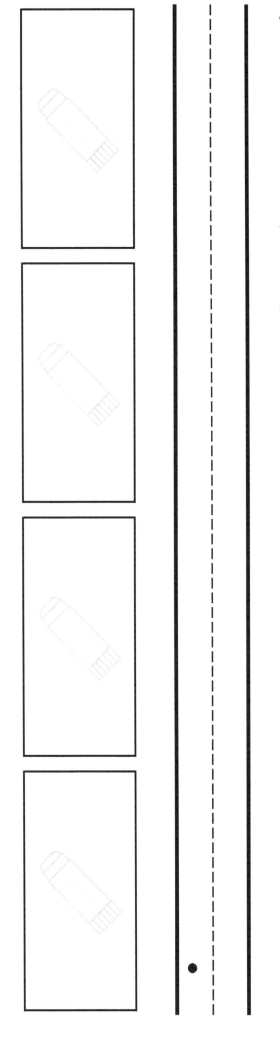

Trace the words on the bottom and then cut them out. Unscramble the words then paste them below to make a sentence.

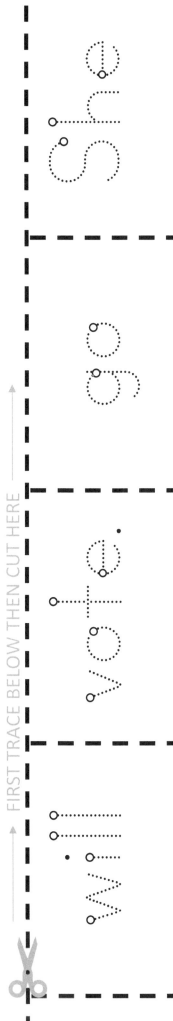

She

go

vote.

Will

Stretch the sentence from the previous page.

She will go vote

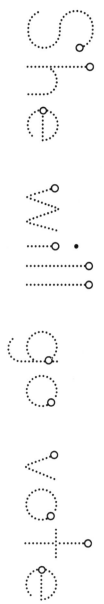

When will she go vote? Copy the phrase and add another detail to make your sentence.

●

_ _ _ _ _ _ _ _ _ _ _ _

☐ Starts with capital letter   ☐ Finger spaces between words   ☐ Ends with a punctuation mark

Optional Prompts:
today.   tomorrow.   next week

Sentence Scrambles

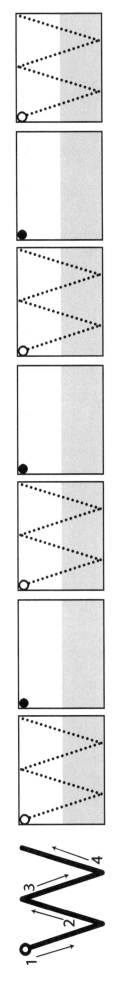

Trace the words on the bottom and then cut them out. Unscramble the words then paste them below to make a sentence.

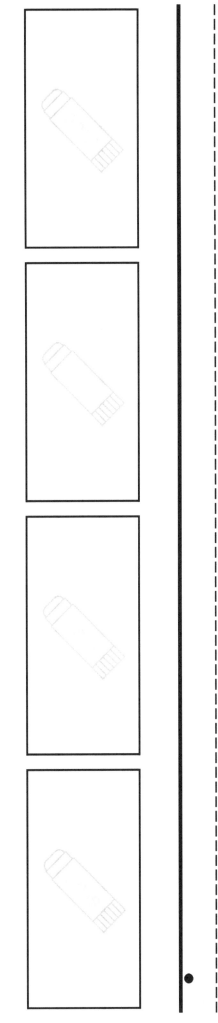

☐ Starts with capital letter ☐ Finger spaces between words ☐ Ends with a punctuation mark

✂ FIRST TRACE BELOW THEN CUT HERE

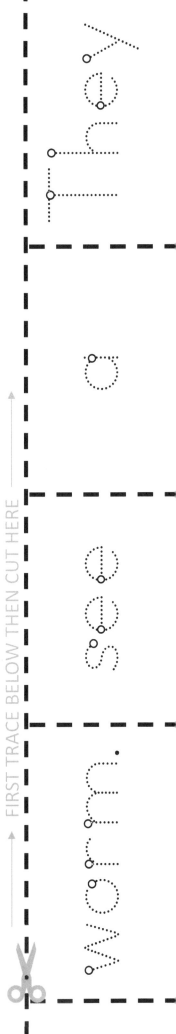

They

a

sees

worm.

SENTENCE STRETCHING

Stretch the sentence from the previous page.

They see a

What word describes the worm? Copy the phrase and add another detail to make your sentence.

• _____

_____

_____

☐ Starts with capital letter   ☐ Finger spaces between words   ☐ Ends with a punctuation mark

Optional Prompts:

little   slimy   wiggly

worm.

Sentence Scrambles

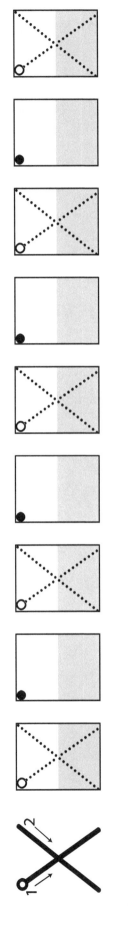

Trace the words on the bottom and then cut them out. Unscramble the words then paste them below to make a sentence.

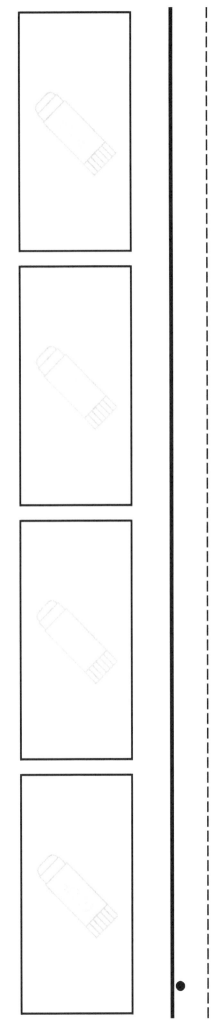

FIRST TRACE BELOW THEN CUT HERE

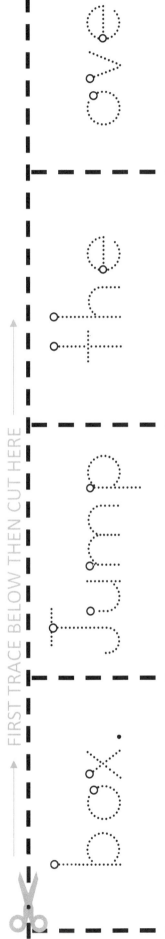

Stretch the sentence from the previous page.

Jump over the _____ box.

● What describes the box? Copy the phrase and add another detail to make your sentence.

_____

_____

_____

☐ Starts with capital letter   ☐ Finger spaces between words   ☐ Ends with a punctuation mark

Optional Prompts:

brown   open   cardboard

Sentence Scrambles

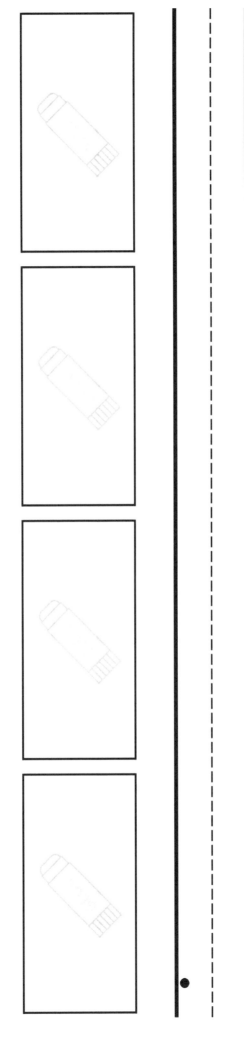

Trace the words on the bottom and then cut them out. Unscramble the words then paste them below to make a sentence.

FIRST TRACE BELOW THEN CUT HERE

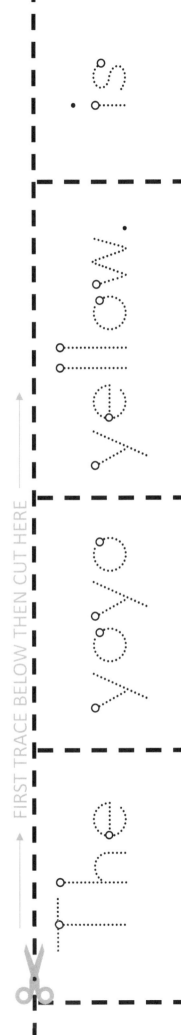

The   yoyo   yellow.   is

SENTENCE STRETCHING

Stretch the sentence from the previous page.

The yoyo is yellow.

What else describes the yoyo? Copy the phrase and add another detail to make your sentence.

The _____

_____

_____

☐ Starts with capital letter   ☐ Finger spaces between words

☐ Ends with a punctuation mark

Optional Prompts:
round   plastic   fun

Sentence Scrambles

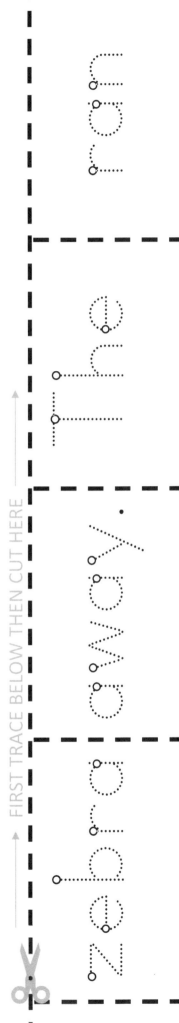

Trace the words on the bottom and then cut them out. Unscramble the words then paste them below to make a sentence.

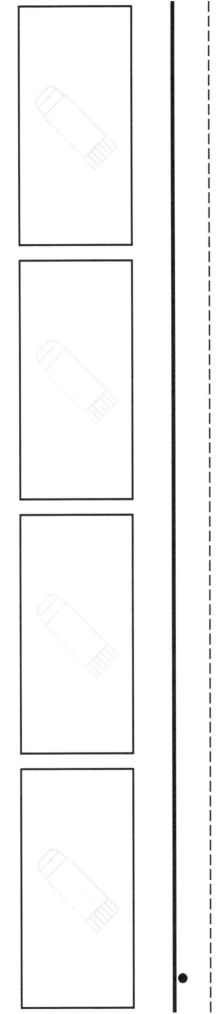

☐ Starts with capital letter ☐ Finger spaces between words ☐ Ends with a punctuation mark

FIRST TRACE BELOW THEN CUT HERE

ran

The

away.

Zebra

SENTENCE STRETCHING

Stretch the sentence from the previous page.

The zebra ran away from a

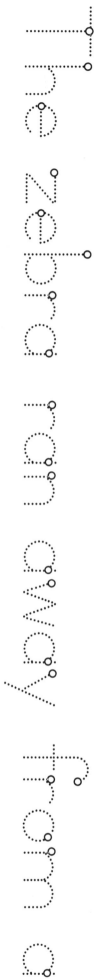

What did the zebra run away from? Copy the phrase and add another detail to make your sentence.

●

_____

_____

☐ Starts with capital letter   ☐ Finger spaces between words   ☐ Ends with a punctuation mark

Optional Prompts:
lion.   bear.   tiger.

Sentence Scrambles

Trace the words on the bottom and then cut them out. Unscramble the words then paste them below to make a sentence.

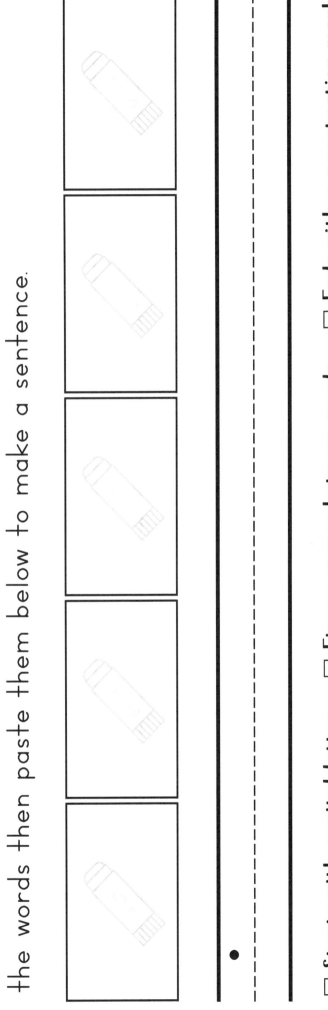

☐ Starts with capital letter ☐ Finger spaces between words ☐ Ends with a punctuation mark

FIRST TRACE BELOW THEN CUT HERE

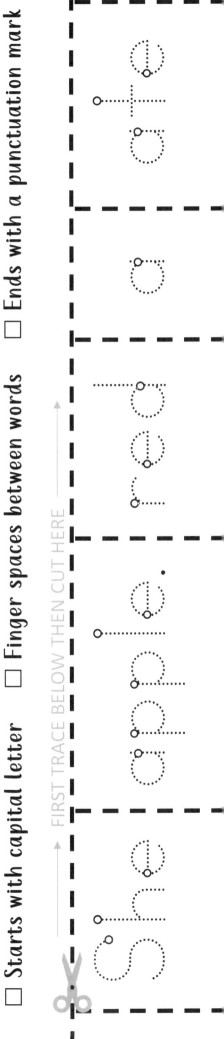

She apples red.

to a

Stretch the sentence from the previous page.

She ate a

What other word describes the **apple?** Copy the phrase and add another detail to make your sentence.

red apple.

☐ **Starts with capital letter**   ☐ **Finger spaces between words**   ☐ **Ends with a punctuation mark**

Optional Prompts:

yummy   crunchy   sour

Sentence Scrambles

Trace the words on the bottom and then cut them out. Unscramble the words then paste them below to make a sentence.

☐ Starts with capital letter   ☐ Finger spaces between words   ☐ Ends with a punctuation mark

✂ FIRST TRACE BELOW THEN CUT HERE

the   likes   bus   He   a blue

SENTENCE STRETCHING

Stretch the sentence from the previous page.

He likes the

What other word describes the bike? Copy the phrase and add another detail to make your sentence.

blue bike.

☐ Starts with capital letter   ☐ Finger spaces between words   ☐ Ends with a punctuation mark

Optional Prompts:
big   new   clean

Sentence Scrambles

Trace the words on the bottom and then cut them out. Unscramble the words then paste them below to make a sentence.

☐ Starts with capital letter ☐ Finger spaces between words ☐ Ends with a punctuation mark

FIRST TRACE BELOW THEN CUT HERE

big is funny My cat

Stretch the sentence from the previous page.

My funny cat is big and

What other word describes the cat? Copy the phrase and add another detail to make your sentence.

☐ Starts with capital letter   ☐ Finger spaces between words   ☐ Ends with a punctuation mark

Optional Prompts:

sneaky.   furry.   quiet.

Sentence Scrambles

Trace the words on the bottom and then cut them out. Unscramble the words then paste them below to make a sentence.

☐ Starts with capital letter   ☐ Finger spaces between words   ☐ Ends with a punctuation mark

→ FIRST TRACE BELOW THEN CUT HERE →

the

Find brown

little duck

SENTENCE STRETCHING

Stretch the sentence from the previous page.

Find the little brown duck

Where is the duck? Copy the phrase and add another detail to make your sentence.

•
- - - - - - - - - - - -
_____
- - - - - - - - - - - -
_____

☐ Starts with capital letter   ☐ Finger spaces between words   ☐ Ends with a punctuation mark

Optional Prompts:
in the water.   in the grass.   at the farm.

Sentence Scrambles

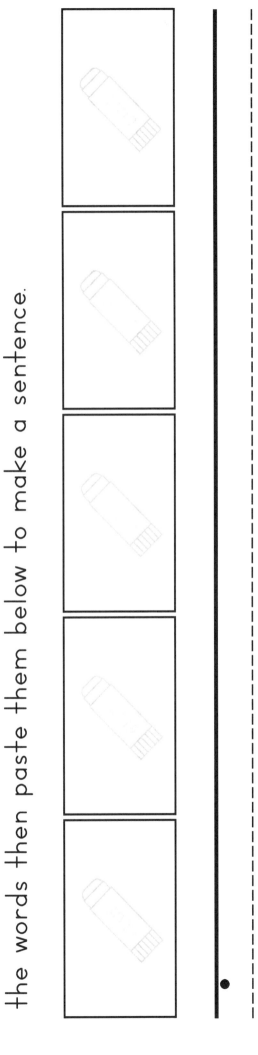

Trace the words on the bottom and then cut them out. Unscramble the words then paste them below to make a sentence.

☐ Starts with capital letter   ☐ Finger spaces between words   ☐ Ends with a punctuation mark

FIRST TRACE BELOW THEN CUT HERE

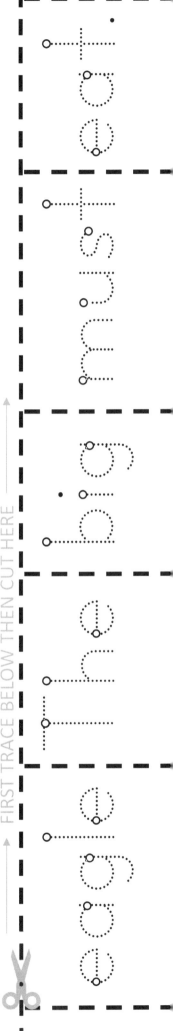

must

big

The

capital

SENTENCE STRETCHING

Stretch the sentence from the previous page.

The big _____ eagle must eat.

What other word describes the eagle? Copy the phrase and add another detail to make your sentence.

-

_____

- - - - - - - - - - - - - - - - - - -

_____

_____

- - - - - - - - - - - - - - - - - - -

☐ **Starts with capital letter**   ☐ **Finger spaces between words**

☐ **Ends with a punctuation mark**

| Optional Prompts: |
| bald   brown   hungry |

Sentence Scrambles

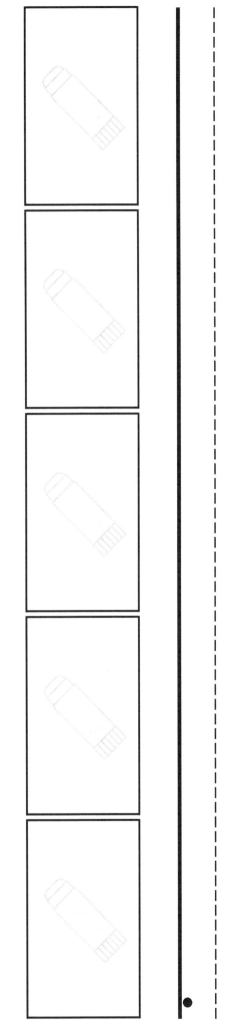

Trace the words on the bottom and then cut them out. Unscramble the words then paste them below to make a sentence.

□ Starts with capital letter   □ Finger spaces between words   □ Ends with a punctuation mark

FIRST TRACE BELOW THEN CUT HERE

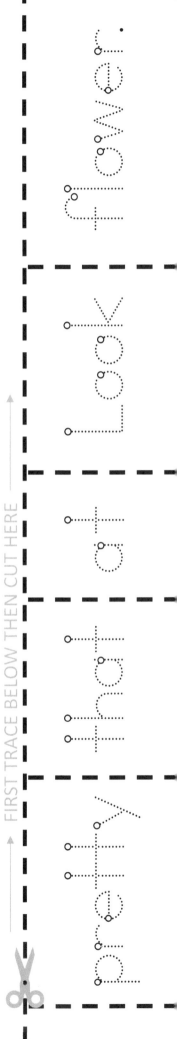

SENTENCE STRETCHING

Stretch the sentence from the previous page.

Look at that pretty flower in the

Where is the flower? Copy the phrase and add another detail to make your sentence.

● _____

☐ **Starts with capital letter**   ☐ **Finger spaces between words**   ☐ **Ends with a punctuation mark**

Optional Prompts:
pot.   garden.   vase.

Sentence Scrambles

Trace the words on the bottom and then cut them out. Unscramble the words then paste them below to make a sentence.

☐ Starts with capital letter   ☐ Finger spaces between words   ☐ Ends with a punctuation mark

→ FIRST TRACE BELOW THEN CUT HERE →

the   ate   Who   all   grapes?

Stretch the sentence from the previous page.

Who ate all the _____ grapes?

What other word describes the grapes? Copy the phrase and add another detail to make your sentence.

☐ **Starts with capital letter**   ☐ **Finger spaces between words**   ☐ **Ends with a punctuation mark**

Optional Prompts:

yummy   green   big

Sentence Scrambles

Trace the words on the bottom and then cut them out. Unscramble the words then paste them below to make a sentence.

FIRST TRACE BELOW THEN CUT HERE

rides
on
She
horse.

Stretch the sentence from the previous page.

She rides on a horse

Where is she riding? Copy the phrase and add another detail to make your sentence.

☐ **Starts with capital letter**   ☐ **Finger spaces between words**   ☐ **Ends with a punctuation mark**

Optional Prompts:

to the barn.   at the farm.   on the road.

Sentence Scrambles

Trace the words on the bottom and then cut them out. Unscramble the words then paste them below to make a sentence.

☐ Starts with capital letter   ☐ Finger spaces between words   ☐ Ends with a punctuation mark

→ FIRST TRACE BELOW THEN CUT HERE →

igloo

in

they

They

went

SENTENCE STRETCHING

Stretch the sentence from the previous page.

They went in the _____ igloo.

What kind of igloo is it? Copy the phrase and add another detail to make your sentence.

☐ **Starts with capital letter**   ☐ **Finger spaces between words**   ☐ **Ends with a punctuation mark**

Optional Prompts:
cold   white   frozen

Sentence Scrambles

Trace the words on the bottom and then cut them out. Unscramble the words then paste them below to make a sentence.

☐ Starts with capital letter   ☐ Finger spaces between words   ☐ Ends with a punctuation mark

← FIRST TRACE BELOW THEN CUT HERE →

juice

like

they

the

Did

SENTENCE STRETCHING

Stretch the sentence from the previous page.

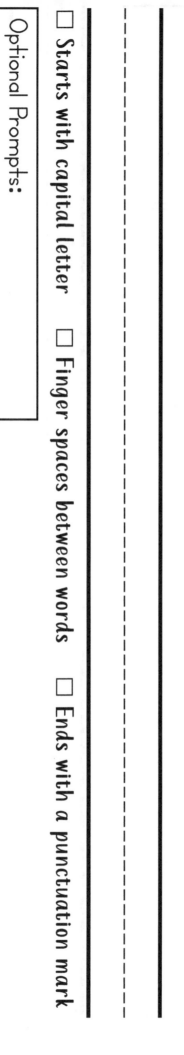

What kind of juice is it? Copy the phrase and add another detail to make your sentence.

_____

- ☐ Starts with capital letter   ☐ Finger spaces between words   ☐ Ends with a punctuation mark

Optional Prompts:

apple   orange   grape

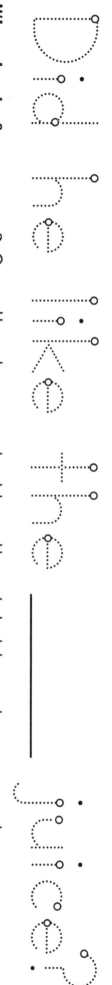

Sentence Scrambles

Trace the words on the bottom and then cut them out. Unscramble the words then paste them below to make a sentence.

☐ Starts with capital letter ☐ Finger spaces between words ☐ Ends with a punctuation mark

FIRST TRACE BELOW THEN CUT HERE

big

The

king

will

eat

Stretch the sentence from the previous page.

The big king will eat

What will the king eat? Copy the phrase and add another detail to make your sentence.

●

☐ Starts with capital letter   ☐ Finger spaces between words   ☐ Ends with a punctuation mark

Optional Prompts:
breakfast.   pizza.   cake.

Sentence Scrambles

Trace the words on the bottom and then cut them out. Unscramble the words then paste them below to make a sentence.

□ Starts with capital letter   □ Finger spaces between words   □ Ends with a punctuation mark

FIRST TRACE BELOW THEN CUT HERE

She

black

lamp.

one

was

SENTENCE STRETCHING

Stretch the sentence from the previous page.

She has one black lamp in the

Where is the lamp? Copy the phrase and add another detail to make your sentence.

●

☐ Starts with capital letter   ☐ Finger spaces between words

☐ Ends with a punctuation mark

Optional Prompts:

room.   corner.   house.

Sentence Scrambles

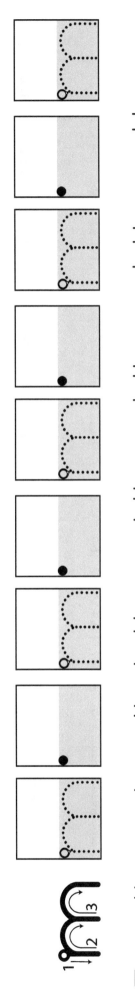

Trace the words on the bottom and then cut them out. Unscramble the words then paste them below to make a sentence.

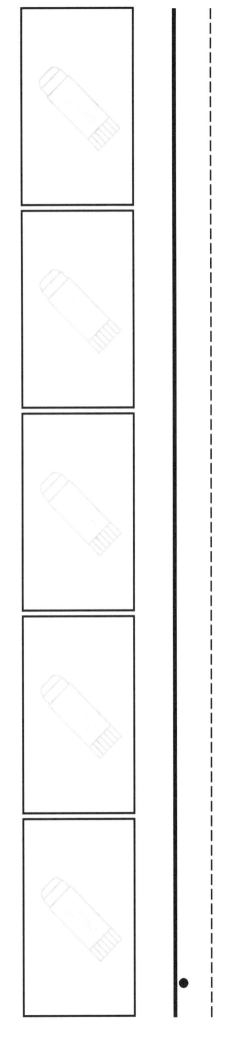

☐ Starts with capital letter   ☐ Finger spaces between words   ☐ Ends with a punctuation mark

← FIRST TRACE BELOW THEN CUT HERE →

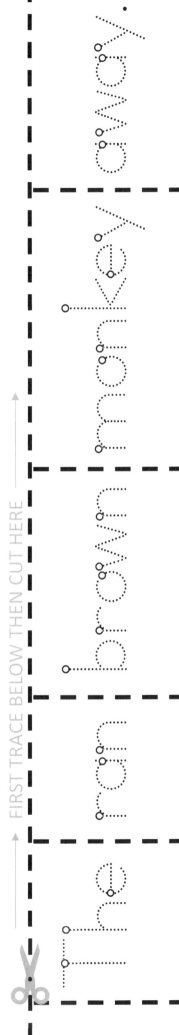

The   ran   brown   monkey   away.

SENTENCE STRETCHING

Stretch the sentence from the previous page.

The brown monkey ran away from the

What did the monkey run away from? Copy the phrase and add another detail to make your sentence.

-

_____

_____

_____

☐ **Starts with capital letter**   ☐ **Finger spaces between words**   ☐ **Ends with a punctuation mark**

Optional Prompts:
gorilla.   lion.   tiger.

Sentence Scrambles

Trace the words on the bottom and then cut them out. Unscramble the words then paste them below to make a sentence.

☐ Starts with capital letter   ☐ Finger spaces between words   ☐ Ends with a punctuation mark

FIRST TRACE BELOW THEN CUT HERE

out

Get

a

I

Will

SENTENCE STRETCHING

Stretch the sentence from the previous page.

I will get a net to catch a

What will you catch with the net? Copy the phrase and add another detail to make your sentence.

•

_____

- - - - - - - - - - - - -

_____

_____

☐ Starts with capital letter   ☐ Finger spaces between words   ☐ Ends with a punctuation mark

Optional Prompts:
butterfly.   fish.   frog.

Sentence Scrambles

Trace the words on the bottom and then cut them out. Unscramble the words then paste them below to make a sentence.

☐ Starts with capital letter ☐ Finger spaces between words ☐ Ends with a punctuation mark

→ FIRST TRACE BELOW THEN CUT HERE

We

sees

a

ox.

brown

SENTENCE STRETCHING

Stretch the sentence from the previous page.

We see a brown ox

Where is the ox? Copy the phrase and add another detail to make your sentence.

☐ Starts with capital letter   ☐ Finger spaces between words   ☐ Ends with a punctuation mark

Optional Prompts:

on the hill.   at the farm.   on the mountain.

Sentence Scrambles

Trace the words on the bottom and then cut them out. Unscramble the words then paste them below to make a sentence.

☐ Starts with capital letter   ☐ Finger spaces between words   ☐ Ends with a punctuation mark

← FIRST TRACE BELOW THEN CUT HERE →

FIRST TRACE BELOW THEN CUT HERE

He   two   has   pigs   pink

SENTENCE STRETCHING

Stretch the sentence from the previous page.

He has two pink pigs and a

What else does he have? Copy the phrase and add another detail to make your sentence.

•

_____

- -

_____

- -

☐ Starts with capital letter   ☐ Finger spaces between words   ☐ Ends with a punctuation mark

Optional Prompts:

cow.   horse.   hen.

Sentence Scrambles

Trace the words on the bottom and then cut them out. Unscramble the words then paste them below to make a sentence.

□ Starts with capital letter □ Finger spaces between words □ Ends with a punctuation mark

FIRST TRACE BELOW THEN CUT HERE

good

queen.

a

Sheena

is

Stretch the sentence from the previous page.

She is a good queen.

What else describes the queen? Copy the phrase and add another detail to make your sentence.

•

_____

_____

_____

☐ Starts with capital letter   ☐ Finger spaces between words   ☐ Ends with a punctuation mark

Optional Prompts:
royal   kind   wise

Sentence Scrambles

Trace the words on the bottom and then cut them out. Unscramble the words then paste them below to make a sentence.

☐ Starts with capital letter   ☐ Finger spaces between words   ☐ Ends with a punctuation mark

FIRST TRACE BELOW THEN CUT HERE

my

Here

rug.

yellow

is.

SENTENCE STRETCHING

Stretch the sentence from the previous page.

Here is my.

yellow rug.

What is your rug like? Copy the phrase and add another detail to make your sentence.

• _____

_____

_____

_____

☐ Starts with capital letter   ☐ Finger spaces between words   ☐ Ends with a punctuation mark

Optional Prompts:

fuzzy   smelly   fluffy

Sentence Scrambles

Trace the words on the bottom and then cut them out. Unscramble the words then paste them below to make a sentence.

☐ Starts with capital letter   ☐ Finger spaces between words   ☐ Ends with a punctuation mark

FIRST TRACE BELOW THEN CUT HERE

snake

there.

under

is

The

Stretch the sentence from the previous page.

The ●●●●● snake is under there.

What word describes the snake? Copy the phrase and add another detail to make your sentence.

● _____

_____

_____

_____

☐ Starts with capital letter   ☐ Finger spaces between words   ☐ Ends with a punctuation mark

Optional Prompts:

slippery   slimy   slithery

Sentence Scrambles

Trace the words on the bottom and then cut them out. Unscramble the words then paste them below to make a sentence.

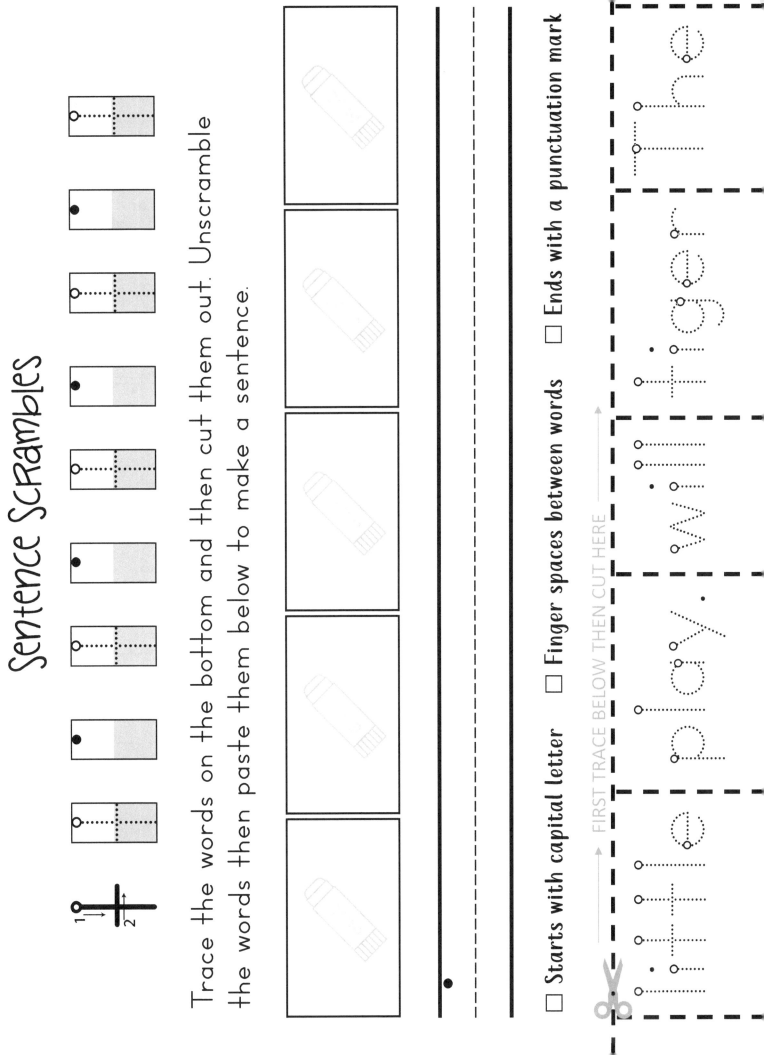

☐ Starts with capital letter ☐ Finger spaces between words ☐ Ends with a punctuation mark

FIRST TRACE BELOW THEN CUT HERE

The play. Will tiger the

SENTENCE STRETCHING

Stretch the sentence from the previous page.

The little tiger will play

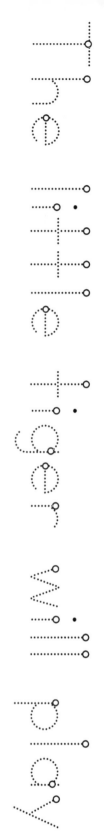

How will the tiger play? Copy the phrase and add another detail to make your sentence.

• _____

_ _ _ _ _ _ _ _ _ _ _ _ _ _ _

_____

_____

_ _ _ _ _ _ _ _ _ _ _ _ _ _ _

☐ Starts with capital letter   ☐ Finger spaces between words   ☐ Ends with a punctuation mark

Optional Prompts:
quietly.   alone.   with friends.

Sentence Scrambles

Trace the words on the bottom and then cut them out. Unscramble the words then paste them below to make a sentence.

□ Starts with capital letter   □ Finger spaces between words   □ Ends with a punctuation mark

✂ FIRST TRACE BELOW THEN CUT HERE

saw   three   black   I   urchins

SENTENCE STRETCHING

Stretch the sentence from the previous page.

I saw three black urchins in the

Where did you see them? Copy the phrase and add another detail to make your sentence.

☐ Starts with capital letter   ☐ Finger spaces between words   ☐ Ends with a punctuation mark

Optional Prompts:
water.   ocean.   fish tank.

Sentence Scrambles

Trace the words on the bottom and then cut them out. Unscramble the words then paste them below to make a sentence.

☐ Starts with capital letter   ☐ Finger spaces between words   ☐ Ends with a punctuation mark

FIRST TRACE BELOW THEN CUT HERE

the

violin.

You

can

play

Stretch the sentence from the previous page.

You can play the violin

When can you play the violin? Copy the phrase and add another detail to make your sentence.

• _____

_____

_____

_____

☐ **Starts with capital letter**   ☐ **Finger spaces between words**   ☐ **Ends with a punctuation mark**

Optional Prompts:

now.   later.   after dinner.

Sentence Scrambles

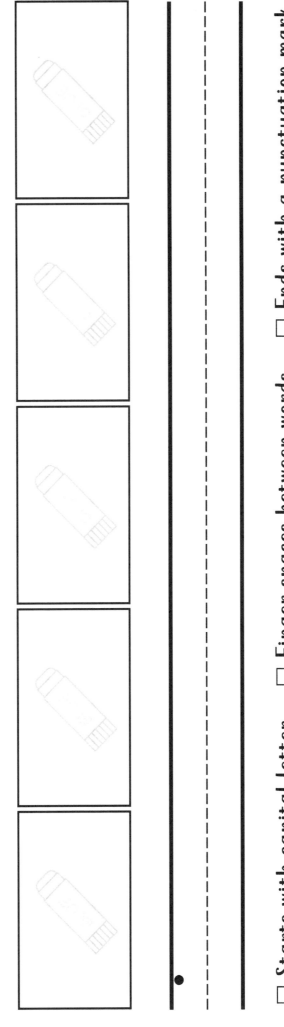

Trace the words on the bottom and then cut them out. Unscramble the words then paste them below to make a sentence.

☐ Starts with capital letter   ☐ Finger spaces between words   ☐ Ends with a punctuation mark

FIRST TRACE BELOW THEN CUT HERE

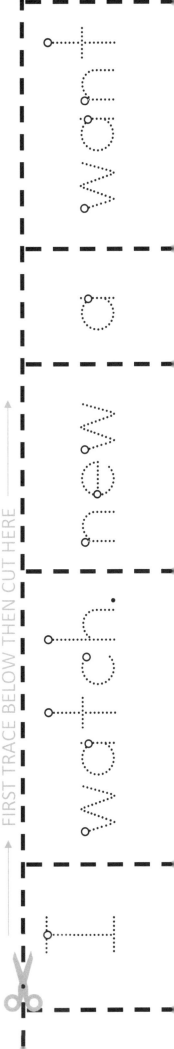

I   watch: new   a   want

Stretch the sentence from the previous page.

I want a new _____ watch.

What kind of watch do you want? Copy the phrase and add another detail to make your sentence.

●

☐ Starts with capital letter   ☐ Finger spaces between words   ☐ Ends with a punctuation mark

Optional Prompts:

wrist   blue   toy

Sentence Scrambles

Trace the words on the bottom and then cut them out. Unscramble the words then paste them below to make a sentence.

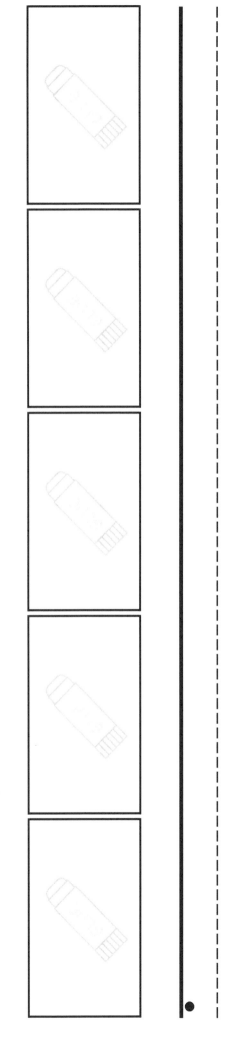

☐ Starts with capital letter   ☐ Finger spaces between words   ☐ Ends with a punctuation mark

← FIRST TRACE BELOW THEN CUT HERE →

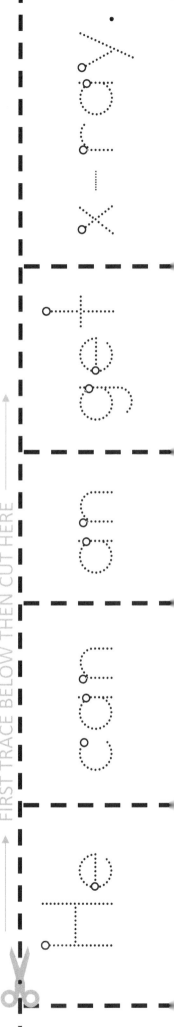

x-ray.

get

an

copy

He

SENTENCE STRETCHING

Stretch the sentence from the previous page.

He can get an x-ray of his

What is he getting x-rayed? Copy the phrase and add another detail to make your sentence.

_____

_____

_____

_____

☐ Starts with capital letter   ☐ Finger spaces between words

☐ Ends with a punctuation mark

Optional Prompts:

arm.   leg.   hand.

Sentence Scrambles

Trace the words on the bottom and then cut them out. Unscramble the words then paste them below to make a sentence.

FIRST TRACE BELOW THEN CUT HERE

☐ Starts with capital letter   ☐ Finger spaces between words   ☐ Ends with a punctuation mark

will

run.

yak

The

big

Stretch the sentence from the previous page.

The big yak will run

Where will the yak run? Copy the phrase and add another detail to make your sentence.

- • _____

_____

_____

_____

☐ Starts with capital letter   ☐ Finger spaces between words   ☐ Ends with a punctuation mark

Optional Prompts:
in the plain.   at the zoo.   to the river.

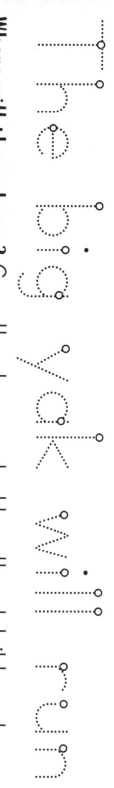

Sentence Scrambles

Trace the words on the bottom and then cut them out. Unscramble the words then paste them below to make a sentence.

□ Starts with capital letter □ Finger spaces between words □ Ends with a punctuation mark

FIRST TRACE BELOW THEN CUT HERE

We

to

zoo.

the

went

SENTENCE STRETCHING

Stretch the sentence from the previous page.

We went to the zoo and saw

What did you see at the zoo? Copy the phrase and add another detail to make your sentence.

☐ Starts with capital letter   ☐ Finger spaces between words   ☐ Ends with a punctuation mark

Optional Prompts:
an elephant.   a giraffe.
a tiger.

Certificate

Congratulations! You've finished Building Sentences Made Fun! You did a great job. Visit our website for a downloadable certificate to celebrate your achievement. Keep up the good work!

We hope you enjoyed the workbook.

Please leave us a review.

Made in United States
Troutdale, OR
05/07/2024

19704762R00064